E

FACTopia!

Follow the TRAIL of 400 FACTS

By KATE HALE

Illustrated by ANDY SMITH

BRITANNICA
BOOKS

CONTENTS

WELCOME TO FACTOPIA!

Time to set off on your adventure through hundreds of mind-blowing, wow-worthy and crazily cool facts. For example...

Did you know that some Roman emperors ate an early form of ice cream? They had ice brought down from the surrounding snowy mountains and flavored it with fruit and juice.

Speaking of mountains... the longest mountain range on Earth is mostly under the sea.

While we're underwater, check out the fact that sea stars have no brains.

Then swim over to the squid, which has a brain all right. It's shaped like a doughnut!

Mmmm, doughnuts. Did you know that Canada has more doughnut shops per person than any other country in the world?

…You might have spotted that there is something special about being here in FACTopia! Every fact is *linked to the next*, and in the most surprising and hilarious ways.

You will follow a trail that takes you from giraffes to the Eiffel Tower to glitter to teeth to quills to feathers to gorillas to… well, you'll see. Discover what each turn of the page will bring!

But there isn't just one trail through this book. Your path branches every now and then, and you can go to a totally different (*but still connected*) part of the book by flipping backward or zooming forward. →

Let your curiosity take you wherever you'd like to go. Of course, a good place to start could be right here, at the beginning

For example, take this detour to find out about speedy things

Go to page 150 ↓

BEFORE THE UNIVERSE BEGAN IT WAS BILLIONS OF TIMES SMALLER THAN THIS DOT.

Newborn babies have about 270 bones. By the time babies grow up, they'll have between 206 and 213 bones.

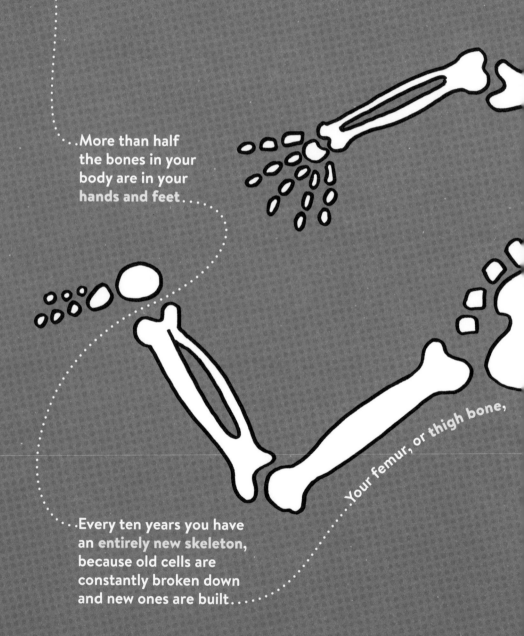

More than half
the bones in your
body are in your
hands and feet.

Your femur, or thigh bone,

Every ten years you have
an entirely new skeleton,
because old cells are
constantly broken down
and new ones are built.

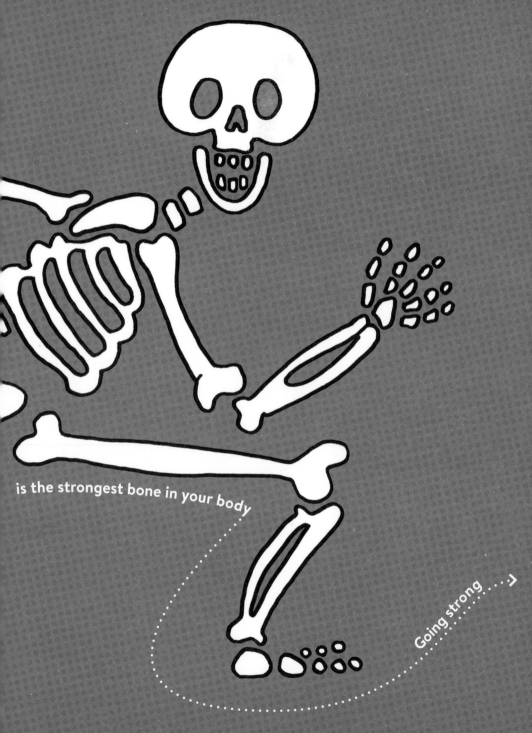

is the strongest bone in your body

Going strong . . . . .

The horned dung beetle is the **world's strongest insect.** It can pull more than 1,141 times its own body weight—that's the same as a person pulling along nearly four-and-a-half double-decker buses

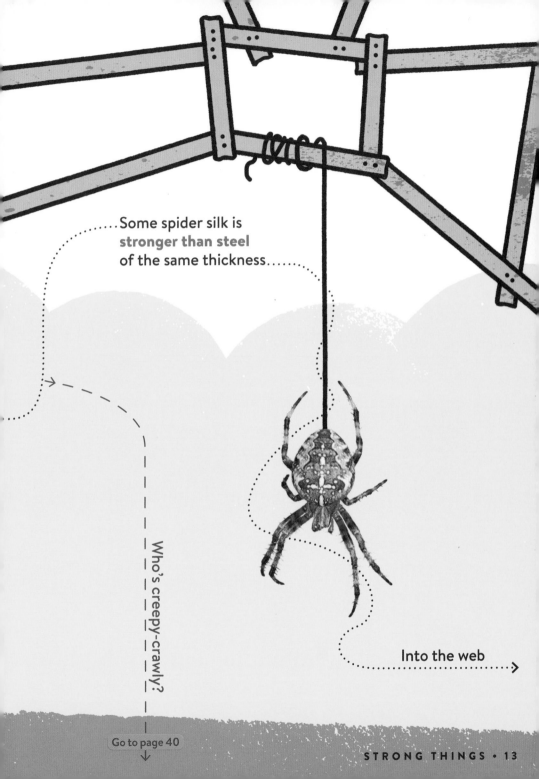

Some spider silk is **stronger than steel** of the same thickness.......

Who's creepy-crawly?

Go to page 40

Into the web →

The diving bell spider lives underwater and breathes using an **air bubble** that it carries around and stores within its web

Triangle weaver spiders fling themselves and their web toward prey like **slingshots**

Some spiders make multiple types of **silk**. Some silks are flexible while others are sticky or strong

Some spiders travel by "ballooning"— they release up to 60 silk threads that spread out to form a "sail" that catches the wind. These spiders have been found soaring hundreds of miles out at sea

Ocean deep…

Some tarantulas can shoot bristly hairs at attackers

Look out!

Go to page 126

The longest mountain range on Earth, the mid-ocean ridge, is mostly under the sea—it's more than 40,000 miles (64,373km) long and eight times longer than the longest mountain range on land, the Andes in South America.

The rings on an adult mountain goat's horns tell you how old it is.

Some people can hear the sound of their eyes moving or their blood flowing.

Earth is not perfectly round. Its shape is called an oblate spheroid, because Earth is squished so that it bulges at the equator.

Owl eyes aren't round, they're tube-shaped.

At the equator, sunsets are faster.

Sunrise or sunset is usually the only time to see a monochrome rainbow, which is completely red.

Red pandas are more closely related to raccoons and skunks than to the black-and-white giant panda.

Male Jackson's chameleons use the three **horns** that grow from their heads to push other males off of **tree** branches.

Firenadoes are a rare type of tornado made of **fire**. These dangerous flaming **winds** can reach speeds of more than 100 miles an hour (160km/h).

Winds on the planet Neptune travel faster than the speed of **sound**.

Giant sequoia **trees** have bark that is **fire** resistant.

Researchers think **panda** poop contains **microscopic** organisms that could help make biofuels.

When in Rome

The ancient Romans used snails to create **purple** dye for their clothes.

Some scientists think the first **microscopic** life on Earth was **purple**.

Salarium, the word ancient Roman soldiers would have used for their wages, comes from the Latin word for

·SALT·

Cha-ching!

Yap, a small Micronesian island, uses **rock discs** with holes in the center as currency. Called rai stones, some weigh more than a car.

Go to page 116

Reeeally big stuff   It's playtime!

The first paper money used in New France (what's now Quebec, Canada) was actually **playing cards**.

In a standard deck of playing cards, the **King of Hearts** is the only king without a mustache.

The tallest **LEGO™ tower** soared nearly 115 feet (35m) high and was built with half a million bricks.

Amazing spaces

Go to page 60

When **Mr. Potato Head**™ was first released, you had to supply your own potato.

The full name of Barbie™ is

Barbara Millicent Roberts.

The Slinky™ was invented accidentally when an engineer was building parts for a ship during World War II.

Whoops!

An 11-year-old invented **the popsicle** after accidentally leaving a wooden stirrer in a sugary liquid outside on a cold night.

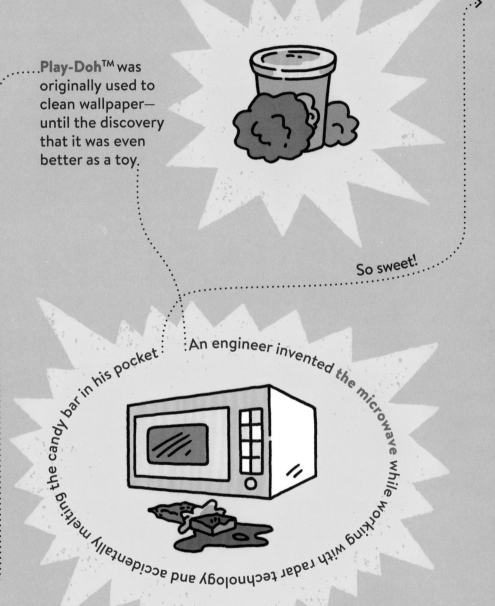

Play-Doh™ was originally used to clean wallpaper—until the discovery that it was even better as a toy.

So sweet!

An engineer invented the microwave while working with radar technology and accidentally melting the candy bar in his pocket.

The world's largest chocolate bar, made in 2020, weighed 5,943 pounds (2,696kg)—that's about the same weight as **four male polar bears**

Chocolate fish are popular treats on **April Fool's Day** in France

Chocolate comes from the beans of the cacao tree. The Mayans and Aztecs thought the beans were **magical** and used them in some of their rituals

Chow down

Go to page 188

Up and away!

The airport in Brussels, Belgium, sells more chocolate than any store on Earth—3 pounds (1.5kg) of chocolate are bought there **every minute**

The average chocolate bar contains some **tiny insect fragments**

....>.... Airplanes leave cloud trails in the sky called "contrails"—they're formed from the water vapor released by the aircraft's engines

A SHEEP, A ROOSTER, AND A DUCK

were the first passengers ever to fly in a hot air balloon.

↑
Go to page 122

Is it a bird?

Rüppell's **griffon vultures** are the world's highest-flying birds. They've been spotted soaring along with airplanes at more than 36,000 feet (10,973m) high

The **largest pterosaur** ever discovered had a wingspan wider than an F-16 fighter jet.

Rain doesn't fall from the sky in the shape of a teardrop—the **water droplets** look more like jellybeans.

Splash!

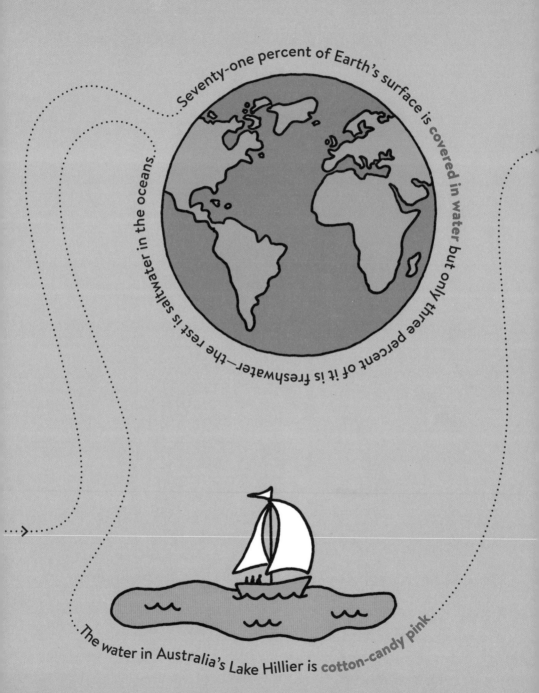

Seventy-one percent of Earth's surface is covered in water but only three percent of it is freshwater—the rest is saltwater in the oceans.

The water in Australia's Lake Hillier is cotton-candy pink.

The Amazon River once flowed
in the opposite direction

The end of a river
is called the mouth.

Go with the flow

The smell of rain when it hits the ground is called petrichor.

The Nile River is the longest river in the world. It flows for more than

What's lurking? >

4,000 miles (6,437km) and through 11 different countries...

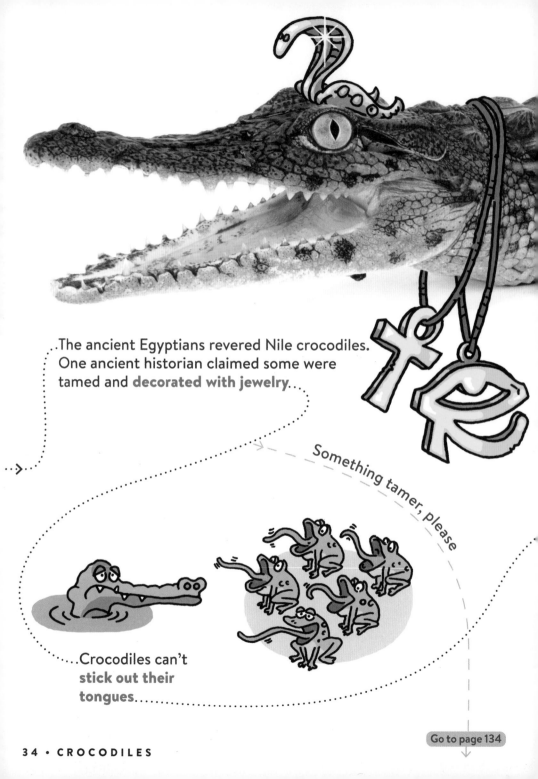

The ancient Egyptians revered Nile crocodiles. One ancient historian claimed some were tamed and **decorated with jewelry.**

Something tamer, please

Crocodiles can't **stick out their tongues.**

Go to page 134

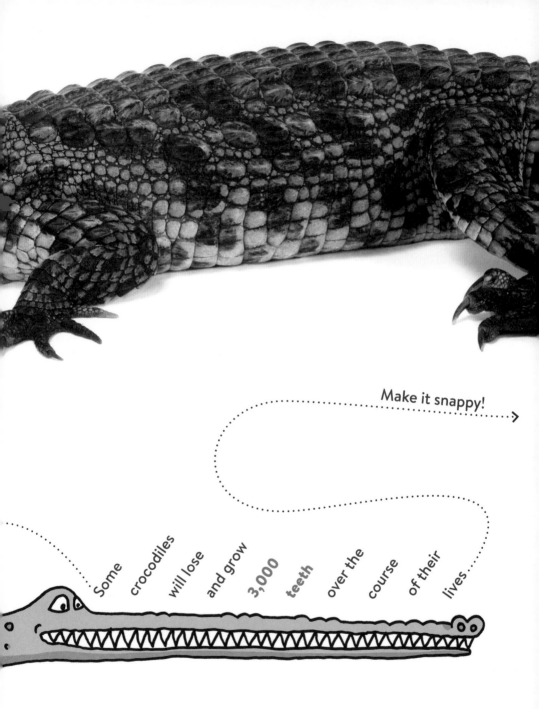

Make it snappy!

Some crocodiles will lose and grow **3,000** teeth over the course of their lives.

The hardest material in the human body is enamel, the coating on your

TEETH.

Say cheese!

Sometimes chimpanzees smile and show their teeth to apologize or to reassure other chimps.

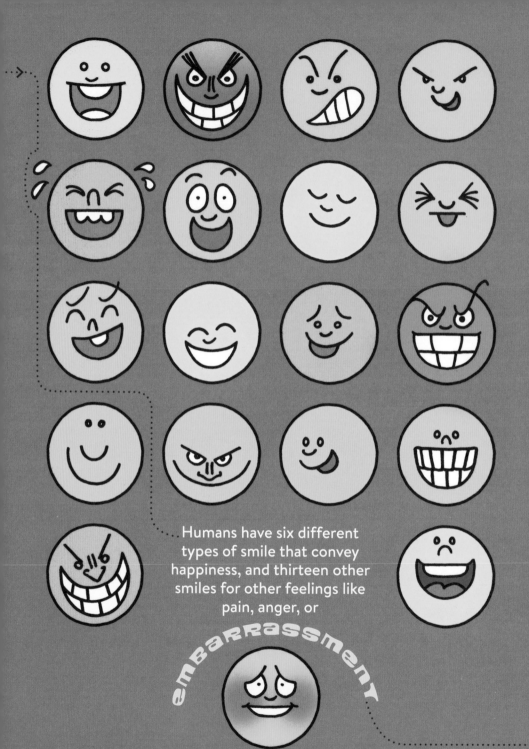

Humans have six different types of smile that convey happiness, and thirteen other smiles for other feelings like pain, anger, or embarrassment

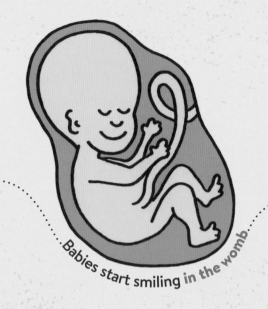

Babies start smiling in the womb.

More bugs →

.The man-faced stink bug is named after the **pattern on its back**, which often looks like a grumpy man's face..............

Dung beetles are able to roll their dung balls **in a straight line** even at night. They use the light from the Milky Way to navigate.

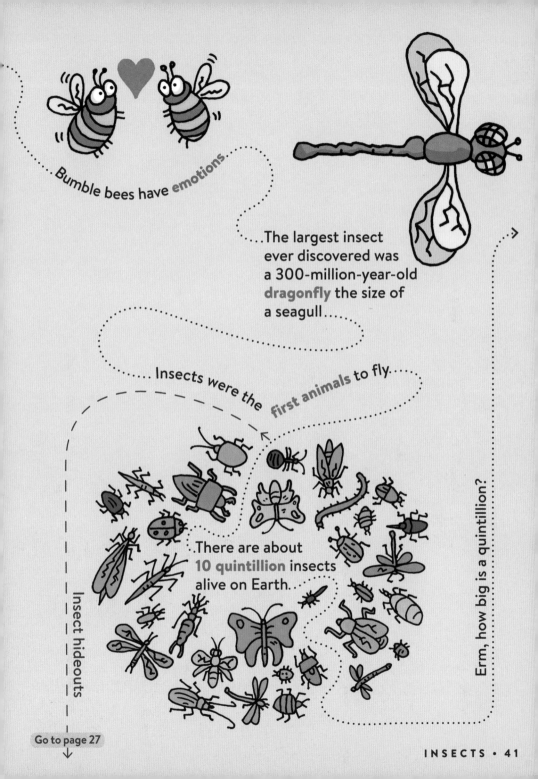

Bumble bees have **emotions**.

The largest insect ever discovered was a 300-million-year-old **dragonfly** the size of a seagull.

Insects were the **first animals** to fly.

There are about **10 quintillion** insects alive on Earth.

Erm, how big is a quintillion?

Insect hideouts

Go to page 27

There are 18 zeros in a quintillion.

About 18 million years ago, our human ancestors had tails.

Some animals use their tails as weapons: Thresher sharks stun their prey by slapping them with their tails.

There's a species of mouse that is immune to the venom of scorpion stings.

There are no words in Spain's national anthem.

When kids lose a tooth in Spain, they put it under their pillow for the tooth mouse, Ratoncito.

Scientists have used snake venom to develop new medicines for people with high blood pressure.

About 2,000 gallons (7,571 liters) of blood are pumped through the average human heart as blood circulates around the body every day.

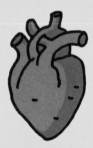

Sharks don't have outer ears, they just have two small holes on top of their heads.

The Hammer Museum in Haines, Alaska, has more than 2,000 hammers on display.

The three smallest bones in your body are in your inner ear and nicknamed the hammer, anvil, and stirrup.

The average dog can understand about 165 words.

Alaska's official state sport is dog mushing.

A golf course in New Mexico has just one tee—it's on the top of a mountain and the hole is at the bottom, more than 2.5 miles (4km) away.

Your heart will beat about 2.5 billion times over the course of your life.

Hole-y moly!

A black hole's gravity is so strong that even light cannot escape it. The smallest black holes are **ten times** the size of our Sun

Blast off!

Go to page 88

Scientists discovered more than **5,000** strange holes on the seafloor off the coast of California. They aren't sure how they got there...........

It's a mystery

No one knows why ancient people created Peru's 2,000-year-old **Nazca Lines.** These massive lines form animals like spiders, hummingbirds, and llamas, or shapes like spirals, straight lines, or trapezoids, and can be seen only from the air.

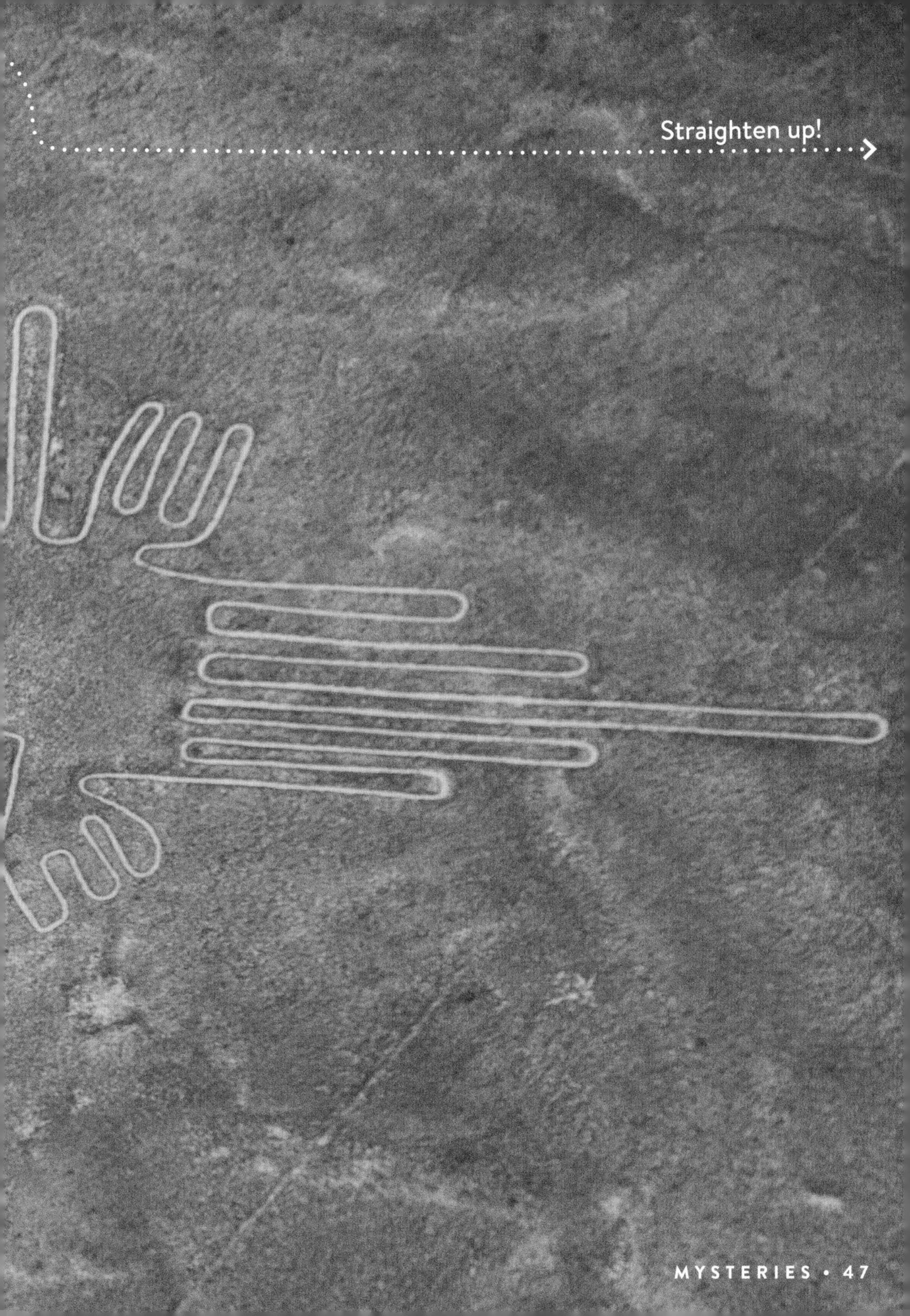

Straighten up!

Part of the U.S.–Canada **border line** runs through the middle of a library.

Two small islands in the Bering Strait are nicknamed "Yesterday" and "Tomorrow" islands. Even though they're only 2.5 miles (4km) apart, they're separated by the **International Date Line**, meaning the time on one island is 24 hours ahead of the other.

Tick tock!

Go to page 152

......The longest line of rubber ducks was over
      1 mile (1.6km) and **17,782 ducks** long...........

......Ants can walk in straight, curved, or zigzag lines
      because they're following **chemical scent trails** left
      by the ants in front of them..................

......If you lined up all the
      Harry Potter books ever
      sold, they would **circle the
      Earth** more than 16 times ....

Round the world we go!

There are thousands of pieces of **space junk**—from old satellites to astronaut gloves—circling the Earth at about 18,000 miles an hour (24,700km/h).

Go to page 150

V-v-vroom!

As well as the Moon, sometimes mini-moons circle the Earth for a few months or even years. These **moonlets** can be about the size of a car and eventually escape Earth's gravitational pull to join asteroids orbiting the Sun...

Every day the International Space Station circles the Earth 16 times......

All aboard!

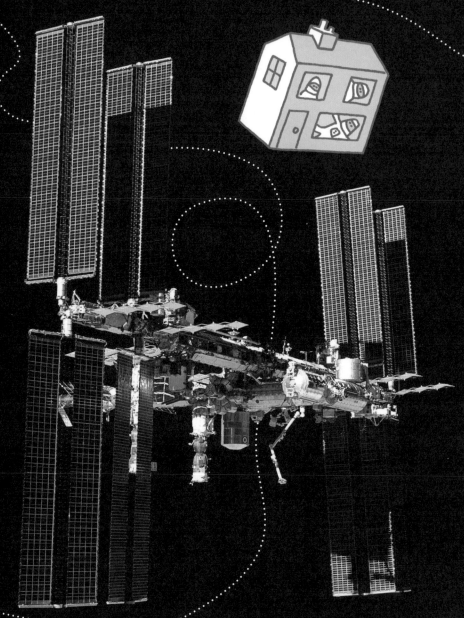

The living space on the INTERNATIONAL SPACE STATION (ISS) is slightly larger than a six-bedroom house.

There are more than 50 computers and over 2.3 million lines of code running on the ISS.

The ISS is the most expensive object ever built.

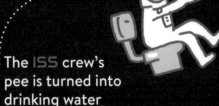

The ISS crew's pee is turned into drinking water

There are three floating robot assistants aboard the ISS called "Astrobees." Their names are Honey, Queen, and Bumble.

Robo-tastic!

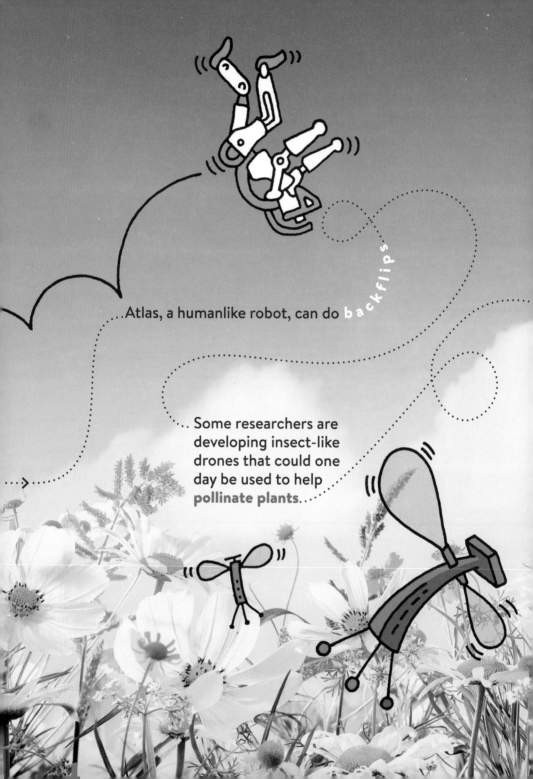

Atlas, a humanlike robot, can do backflips.

Some researchers are developing insect-like drones that could one day be used to help **pollinate plants**.

Animal mechanics

The **first robot** was created more than 2,000 years ago in ancient Greece. It was a mechanical wooden dove.

Go to page 24

Scientists studied fireflies to design a new, brighter **LED** light bulb

Engineers modeled **bullet trains** off of a kingfisher's beak to make them quieter and more efficient. Kingfishers dive into the water to catch their prey almost silently and without splashing

Termites create giant mounds that can be taller than a giraffe and have a natural heating and cooling system. Architects are looking to termites when designing new energy-efficient buildings....

Beastly builders

The world's largest **beaver dam** is located in Alberta, Canada, and is so massive it can be seen by satellites in space. The beavers in the area have been constructing it since the 1970s

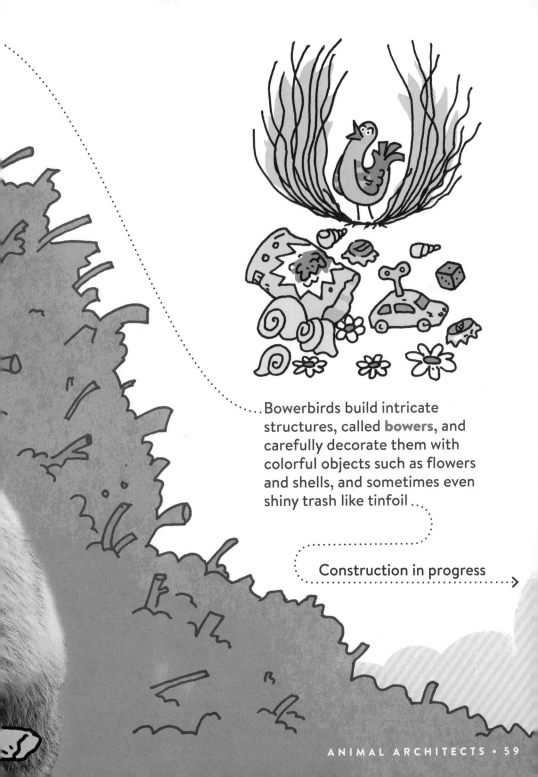

Bowerbirds build intricate structures, called **bowers**, and carefully decorate them with colorful objects such as flowers and shells, and sometimes even shiny trash like tinfoil ...

Construction in progress

Employees in India's fisheries department headquarters work in an office

At the Big Idaho Potato Hotel, rooms are located inside a giant 6-ton (5,443kg) replica of a **potato**.

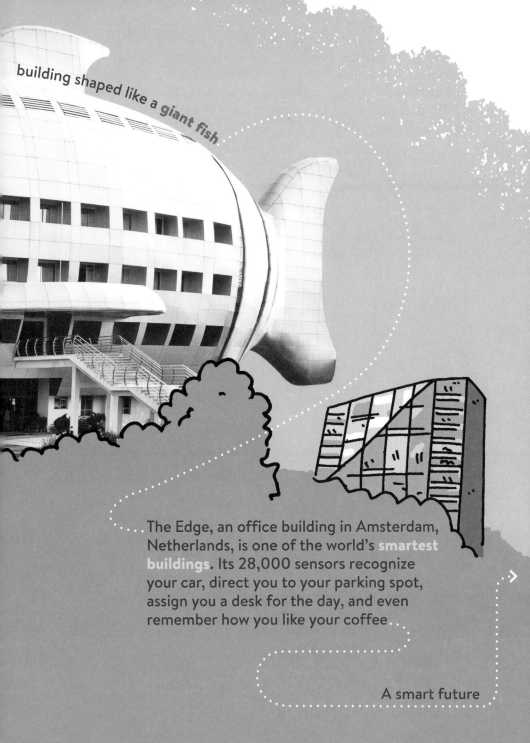

building shaped like a giant fish

The Edge, an office building in Amsterdam, Netherlands, is one of the world's **smartest buildings**. Its 28,000 sensors recognize your car, direct you to your parking spot, assign you a desk for the day, and even remember how you like your coffee.

A smart future

Some predict that one day people living in cities could be riding to work

Engineers are working on **smart watches** that wouldn't be powered by batteries, but by human sweat.

When you head to a sports stadium for the big game, you might see **holographic replays** and get a personal video feed so you never miss the action by your favorite player.

Companies are designing **smart clothes** like shirts that can track your heart rate, socks that analyze your running style, and jackets that can interact with apps.

Get dressed!

and school on giant drones

Go to page 128

Take a big sniff

Ancient Egyptians wore wax **cone-shaped hats** that melted during the day and made the wearer smell fragrant...

Italian women in the 16th century wore **platform shoes** called "chopines" that were so high the women had to walk with an attendant so they didn't fall over...

······ French queen Marie Antoinette once styled a **model ship** into her hair to celebrate winning a battle at sea ·······

Queen **Cleopatra** of Egypt was said to coat her boat's sails with strong-smelling perfume

Among Queen **Elizabeth II**'s many titles is "Seigneur of the Swans," which means all unowned mute swans in the U.K. technically belong to her

Some **Inca emperors** wore clothing made of bat fur

Greek king **Alexander the Great** named a city Bucephala, after his favorite horse

To the castle!

Chinese Emperor **Qin Shihuangdi** was buried with an army of around 8,000 terra-cotta soldiers.

Disneyland's Sleeping Beauty Castle was inspired by Germany's **Neuschwanstein Castle**.

Japan's **Himeji Castle** had 84 different gates. Some led to dead ends to confuse attackers.

Syria's **Krak des Chevaliers Castle** had a defensive wall almost 100 feet (30m) thick

Predjama Castle

in Slovenia is built into the entrance of a cave and has a system of secret passages

The world's **tallest sandcastle** measured 57 feet (18m) high, and was built with turrets and knights, and a dragon at its base

Unbelievable!

Explorer Marco Polo thought he had stumbled upon **unicorns** during his travels—they were actually rhinoceroses...

Christopher Columbus claimed to have spotted **mermaids** on his journey to the Americas—but they were probably manatees...

More animal tricksters

Go to page 138

Go to page 126

Attaaack!

Instead of squirting ink like most species of squid, the **vampire squid** shoots a glowing mucus at would-be attackers.

Dracula ants

have the fastest bite of any animal on the planet—they can chomp down 5,000 times faster than you can blink.

Goblin sharks can extend their jaws outward to the tip of their long nose, then retract them, to help them quickly attack their prey.

Flying dragon lizards use flaps of skin on their sides as sails to glide through the air. They steer using their tails....

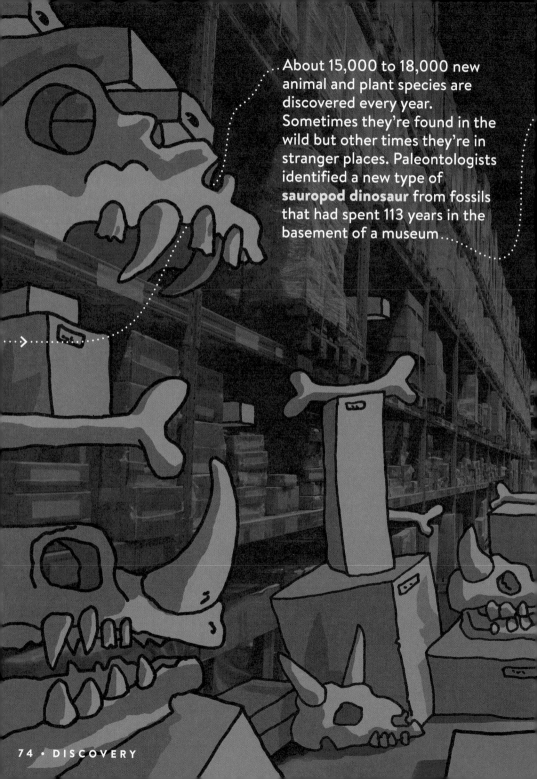

About 15,000 to 18,000 new animal and plant species are discovered every year. Sometimes they're found in the wild but other times they're in stranger places. Paleontologists identified a new type of **sauropod dinosaur** from fossils that had spent 113 years in the basement of a museum

There's a museum in Texas that features more than 1,400 art pieces—all created on **toilet seats**.

An owl can turn its **head** further than any other animal—270 **degrees** each way.

The barreleye is a fish with a **see**-through **head**.

A college gave an honorary **degree** in veterinary medicine to Moose, an eight-year-old therapy **dog**.

An African wild **dog** has only four toes on each **paw**—all other dogs have five.

A jewelry company made a **toilet seat** set with 40,815 **diamonds**, a world record.

Some **diamonds** are almost as old as the **Earth** itself.

Basketballs weren't always **orange**. They were originally brown, but they were changed so players and fans could **see** them better.

Earth's early atmosphere caused our planet to look **orange** from space.

Flower power

The kangaroo **paw** plant is named after its flowers, which look like kangaroo claws.

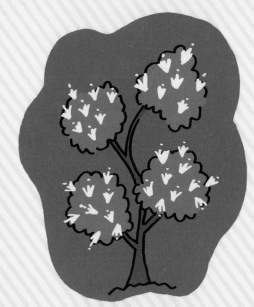

The largest flower blooms from the **Rafflesia** plant, or "monster flower," found in Southeast Asia. It can weigh as much as a terrier and its opening is big enough to fit a baby inside.

BALSA TREES
flower at night

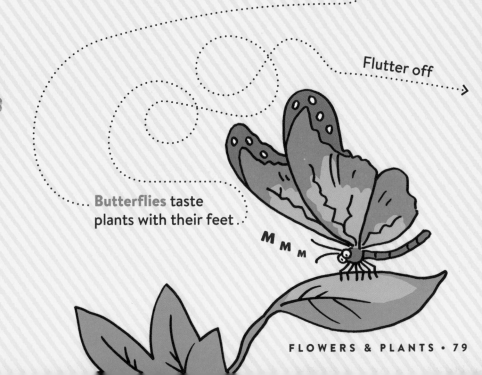

Flutter off

Butterflies taste plants with their feet

M M M

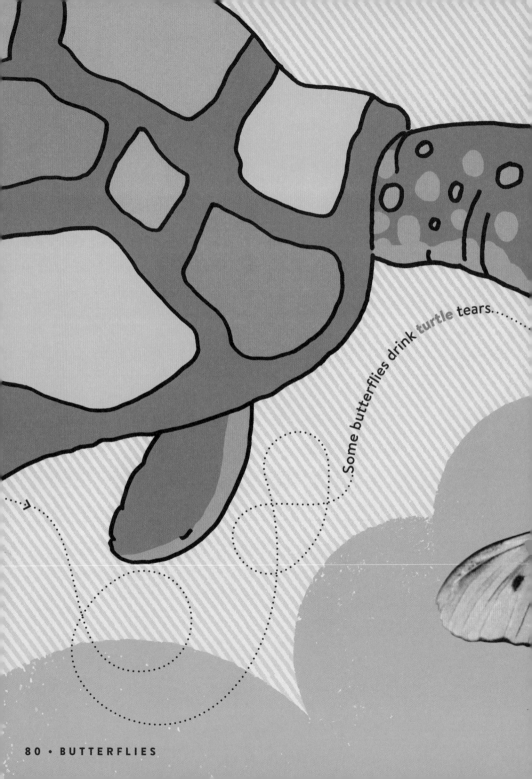

Some butterflies drink *turtle* tears.

Monarch butterflies migrate from Mexico to Canada each year. It takes the butterflies up to five generations to travel that far—so some of the insects that complete the migration are the **great-great-grandchildren** of the butterfly that started the journey.

Pack your bags!

Animals migrate to **find resources**, like food or water, that they wouldn't have if they stayed in one place

The bar-tailed godwit flies 7,000 miles (11,265km) on its annual migration from **Alaska to New Zealand**, sometimes without ever stopping

People on Australia's Christmas Island built bridges and tunnels so the 50 million red crabs that migrate from the forests to the ocean each year have a **safe route** to travel.

Time for a vacation

Birds that migrate long distances sleep while flying. Some species take **12-second naps** throughout the day.

Millions of golden jellyfish migrate each day across a lake in Palau, an island in the South Pacific, as they follow the **Sun's rays**. The light nourishes the algae that live inside the jellyfish, which in turn provide food for the jelly.

Yaaawwn!

Go to page 156

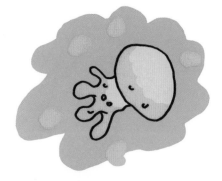

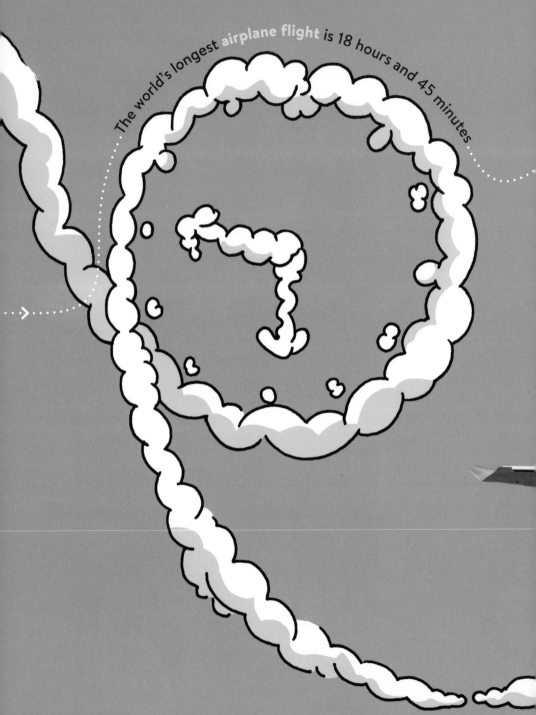

The world's longest airplane flight is 18 hours and 45 minutes

Tourists may soon be able to stay at the **International Space Station** for the price of $35,000 per night (not including rocket-ship fees)

It's all rocket science

FALCON HEAVY,

the world's most powerful rocket, has 27 engines, which generate the same amount of thrust as about 18 aircraft engines.......

Houston, we have liftoff!

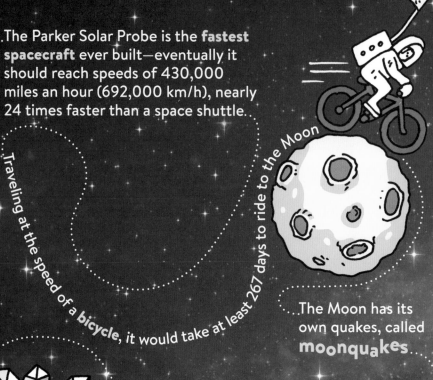

The Parker Solar Probe is the **fastest spacecraft** ever built—eventually it should reach speeds of 430,000 miles an hour (692,000 km/h), nearly 24 times faster than a space shuttle.

Traveling at the speed of a **bicycle**, it would take at least 267 days to ride to the Moon

The Moon has its own quakes, called **moonquakes**

People have discovered **diamonds** on Earth that came from a planet that no longer exists in our solar system

The **farthest star** we've ever observed was about 9 billion light-years away.

Temperatures on Venus can reach nearly 900°F (480°C)—that's **hot enough** to melt lead

More facts that sizzle

Go to page 172

A meteor is the bright streak of light that can be seen when a meteoroid enters Earth's atmosphere. A meteor that appears brighter than Venus is called a **fireball**

THE SPACECRAFTS VOYAGERS 1 AND 2 HAVE BEEN TRAVELING THROUGH SPACE SINCE 1977 AND ARE MORE THAN 11 BILLION MILES (17.7 BILLION KM) AWAY FROM OUR SUN. THEY WON'T ENCOUNTER ANY OTHER STARS FOR AT LEAST 40,000 YEARS

Light travels from the Sun to Earth in 8 minutes and 20 seconds

A day on Jupiter is only about **10 hours**

Researchers think more than 48 tons (44,000kg) of rocks from space hit Earth each day. Some are only the size of a **speck of dust**

We can go bigger

The space rock that hit Earth and brought about the **extinction** of most of the dinosaurs was an asteroid about 7.5 miles (12km) wide—that's the same as 1,131 school buses lined up end to end.

Scientists think dinosaurs may have **danced** to attract mates like birds do today.

Tampa, Florida, is home to **Recyclosaurus**, a 25-foot-tall (7.6m-tall) *Tyrannosaurus rex* sculpture made of recycled material. Even its skin is recycled—it's made of orange construction fencing.

Scientists have discovered dinosaur fossils on every continent —even Antarctica

Egg-cellent!

Some dinosaurs laid **blue** eggs.

...Most bird eggs start out **white**, but as they develop some turn shades of **brown**, **green**, **blue**, and even **black**...

...The color of a chicken's **earlobe** often determines what color its eggs will be...

Go to page 160

More color, please

The winner of the

THE

WORLD
HARD-BOILED
EGG EATING
CHAMPIONSHIP

downed 141 eggs
in 8 minutes.

Yum yum!

Every year contestants in Oatman, Arizona, try to **fry an egg** on the sidewalk using only the heat from the Sun.

Astronauts on board Apollo 11, the first spacecraft to land on the Moon, took **Kellogg's Corn Flakes** into space, but they brought them back to Earth uneaten...

A traditional breakfast in Morocco often includes *baghrir*, also known as "thousand-hole pancakes."

Take a coffee break

In the Netherlands, breakfast sometimes includes bread sprinkled with **chocolate pieces** called *hagelslag*, or "hailstorm"...

...**Coffee beans** are actually seeds of the coffee cherry, a type of fruit...

More holes...

Go to page 44

Legend says that a goatherd from Ethiopia discovered coffee after

noticing how energized his **goats** were after eating the plant.

Goats' pupils are shaped like **rectangles**.

A **rectangle** has four sides.

Quill writing pens were made from only the five largest of a goose or swan's wing **feathers**.

Famous Roman author Pliny the Elder cleaned his **teeth** with a porcupine **quill**.

Fluoride is a **mineral** that comes from rocks. It's found in toothpaste and helps protect your **teeth**.

The largest known dinosaur with **feathers** was a 23-foot-long (7m-long) tyrannosaur that weighed as much as 10 male **gorillas**.

Gorilla nose prints are like human fingerprints—no two are the same.

There are **four** different species of **giraffe**.

A group of **giraffes** is called a **tower**.

Ancient cave artists used **paint** with glitter—in the form of a shimmery, crushed-up **mineral** called mica—in their art.

Every seven years, the Eiffel **Tower** receives about 60 tons (54,000kg) worth of fresh **paint**.

The human **nose** can detect one trillion *different scents.*

Bactrian camels are able to smell the **scent** of certain water **bacteria**, allowing the camels to locate water from up to 50 miles (80km) away.

You could find more than a billion **bacteria** in just a teaspoon (1g) of dirt.

Dig down

Tall **prairie grasses** can have 14-foot-long (4m-long) root systems that extend into the dirt.

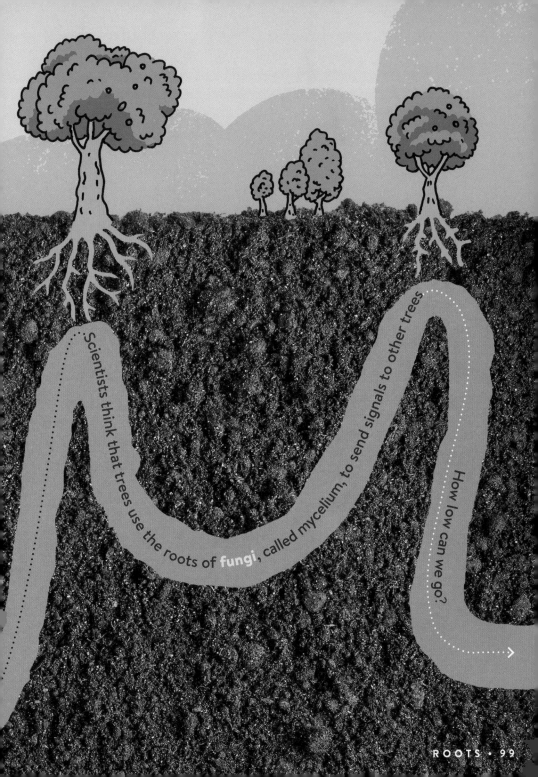

Scientists think that trees use the roots of **fungi**, called mycelium, to send signals to other trees.

How low can we go?

Some mole rats communicate with one another

An old salt mine in Romania was turned into an underground **amusement park** complete with a bowling alley, mini-golf course, and a Ferris wheel

by **banging** their heads against their tunnel walls.

Earthworms don't have legs, but their bodies are covered in teeny tiny **bristles** called setae that help them move and dig.

The **center of the Earth** is 1,800 miles (2,900km) below the surface—that's the same as about 327 Mount Everests stacked on top of one another

Some types of melted underground rock, or **magma**, can reach temperatures nearly three times as hot as the surface of Mercury

So fiery

Pieces of lava that fly through the air from an erupting volcano and are still molten when they land are called **spatter**

The **loudest** sound ever recorded was from the eruption of Indonesia's Krakatoa volcano in 1883. It was so loud that sound waves from the explosion circled the Earth up to four times

There's a restaurant on Spain's Canary Islands that **uses heat** from a volcano to cook its food

Instead of sitting on their eggs, some species of birds **bury** their eggs in volcanic ash and use the volcano's heat to keep them warm

Get cracking!

Go to page 92

A volcano in Tanzania has lava that flows black or sometimes **silvery** because it contains a special rock called carbonatite

That rocks!

Salt is the only rock humans eat

Uluru, an enormous sandstone rock in Australia's desert, was under an ocean four hundred million years ago.

Geodes are hollow rocks with crystals inside. Most are small enough to hold in your hand, but one of the largest ever discovered is 26 feet (8m) long with crystals the size of a person.

Treasures this way

Go to page 136

Strike gold

The **Bactrian hoard** uncovered in Afghanistan is one of the largest treasure troves ever discovered. It contained gold jewelry and weapons, and a crown made of gold so thin that the headpiece could be folded up.......................

Most pirates didn't bury their treasure. One of the few accounts of it happening was by **Captain William Kidd**, who buried his booty off the coast of New York's Long Island......... Ahoy! Me hearties!

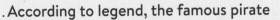

According to legend, the famous pirate

BLACKBEARD

lit fuses under his hat to scare his enemies...........

Many pirate ships had a set of laws called the **"Pirate Code,"** which crewmates had to follow. One code set an 8 p.m. curfew.

Follow the rules >

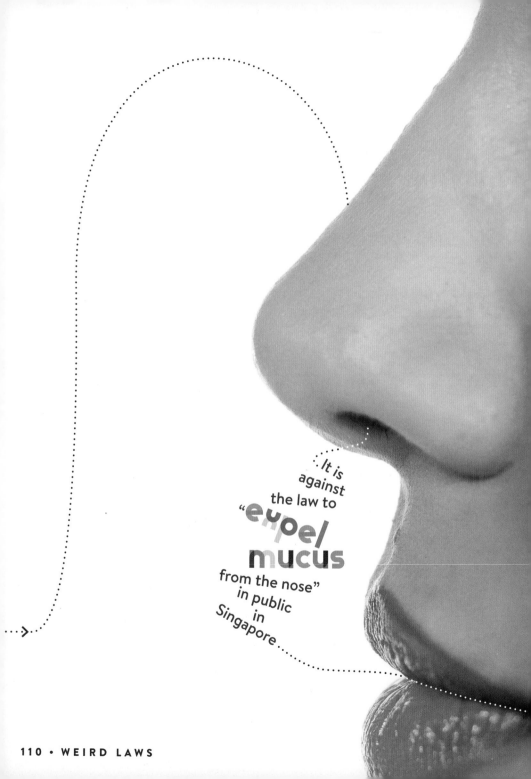

It is against the law to "expel mucus from the nose" in public in Singapore

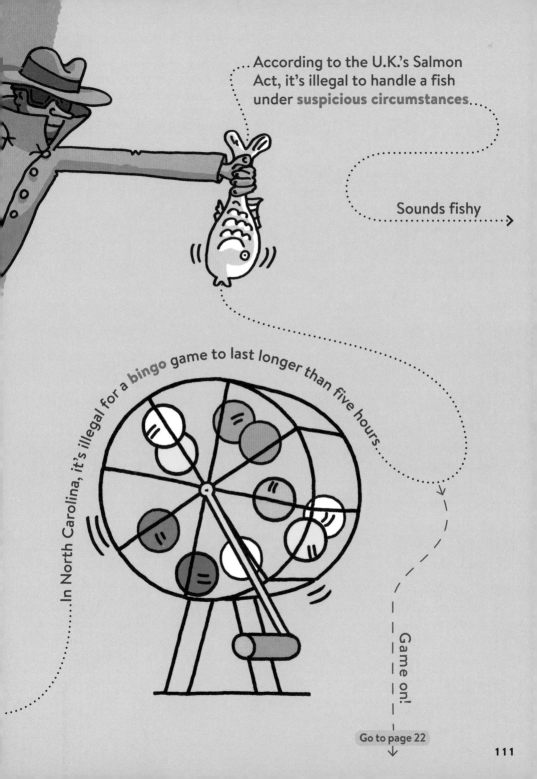

According to the U.K.'s Salmon Act, it's illegal to handle a fish under **suspicious circumstances**.

Sounds fishy

In North Carolina, it's illegal for a **bingo** game to last longer than five hours.

Game on!

Go to page 22

There are more types of fish on **Earth** than all the different species of reptiles, mammals, birds, and amphibians combined.

The center of the **Earth** is a ball of solid metal.

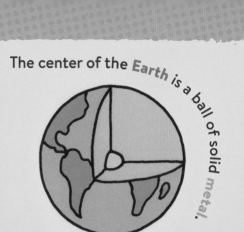

There are about 70 plastic **houses** shaped like **UFOs** all over the world.

Some estimate it would take up to 23.5 million helium-filled party **balloons** to lift a small **house** into the air.

There's an official **UFO** landing pad in Alberta, **Canada**.

Canada has more **doughnut** shops per person than any other country in the world.

The metal gallium will **M E L T** in your **hand**.

A 36-foot (11m) left-hand sculpture rises out of the sand in Chile's Atacama Desert.

Artist Jeff Koons creates **sculptures** of giant **balloon** dogs out of stainless steel—one sold for nearly $60 million.

Squid-gy!

The giant squid has a brain shaped like a **doughnut**—the squid's throat goes right through the middle.

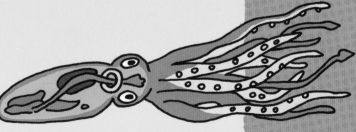

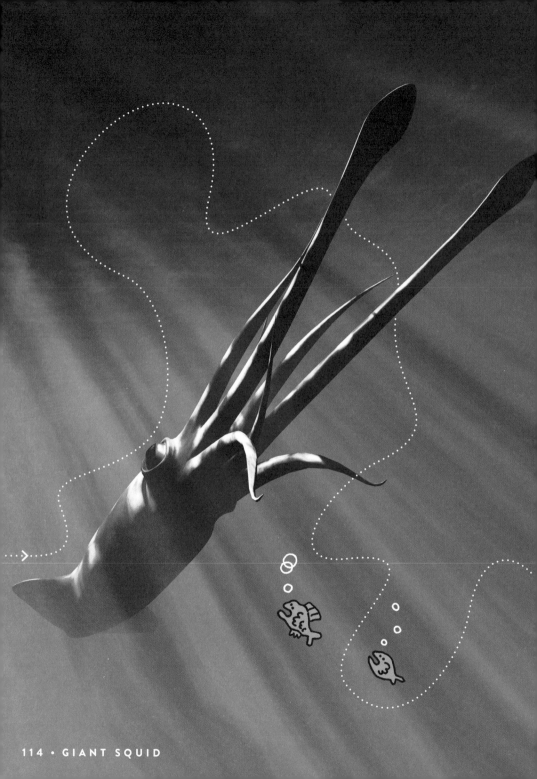

Giant squid have the largest eyes of any animal—they're the size of dinner plates

From biggest

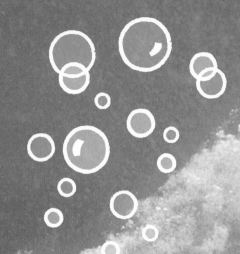

A blue whale's tongue can equal the weight of an elephant

The biggest mountain in the solar system is on Mars. Called **Olympus Mons**, it stretches 14 miles (22km) high, about two-and-a-half times taller than Mount Everest........

To smallest

>

...Bee hummingbirds lay eggs the size of coffee beans...

The smallest living thing is a type of bacteria so small that

**150,000**

could fit on the end of a human hair.

Pack it in! →

Scientists call some strains of **bacteria** that swarm together and hunt other types of bacteria a "wolf pack".

When **sea otters** rest, they float together in the water holding each others' paws or feet. Some sea otter "rafts" are made up of more than 1,000 otters joined together.

A group of pugs is called a

GRUMBLE

Go to page 14

Tangled webs

Some spider colonies can be home to over 50,000 spiders

A group of owls is called a

Parliament

Twit-twoo!

...Owls can **swallow** their prey whole

Peregrine falcons can **dive** at speeds of about 200 miles an hour (322km/h)—faster than the average speed of a Formula One race car...

The biggest bird's **nest** ever discovered was over 9 feet (2.7m) wide. Built by two bald eagles, it weighed nearly 4,500 pounds (2,000kg)—more than a car...

Scientists think that some birds of prey's eyes are so powerful they can **see** Earth's magnetic field...

I spy

In front of a hotel in Dallas, Texas, stands a 30-foot-tall (9.1m-tall) eyeball modeled after the artist's own blue eyes

Peacock mantis shrimp have **16** color receptors in their eyes—humans have only three.

Horned lizards can **shoot blood** from their eyes at predators

Fire!

Build some more

Go to page 60

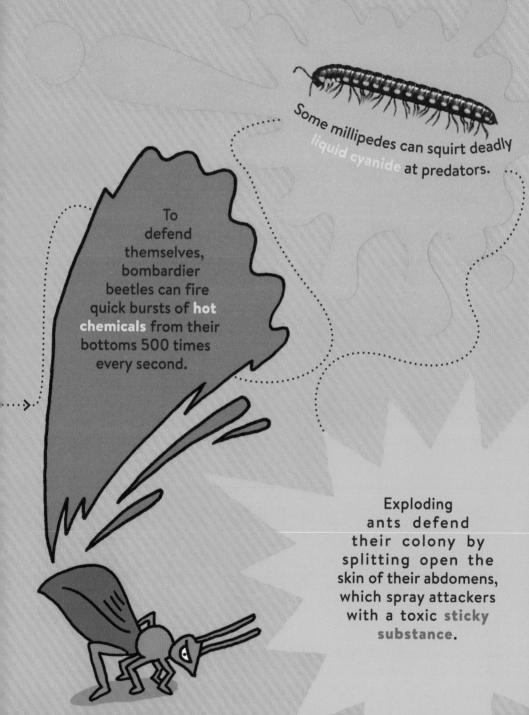

Some millipedes can squirt deadly liquid cyanide at predators.

To defend themselves, bombardier beetles can fire quick bursts of **hot chemicals** from their bottoms 500 times every second.

Exploding ants defend their colony by splitting open the skin of their abdomens, which spray attackers with a toxic **sticky substance**.

Hagfish are eel-like animals that can produce four cups of **slime** in under a second. The slime can get into a predator's gills, choking it.

When threatened, honey badgers release a "STINK BOMB" from their bottoms.

Pe-eww!

Hoatzins are nicknamed "stink birds" because they smell like **poop**. The stench is so strong that it drives away predators

Go to page 78

So flowery!

Off we pop!

Corpse Flowers

smell like **rotting meat** in order to attract insects

Binturongs, tree-climbing mammals from Southeast Asia, smell like **popcorn**.

ANCIENT PEOPLE IN PERU ATE POPCORN—ARCHAEOLOGISTS HAVE FOUND POPCORN COBS THEY THINK COULD BE UP TO 6,000 YEARS OLD.

Viva Peru!

Visitors to Peru can sleep in **glass** pods that dangle off the side of a cliff.

A type of **glass** called a fulgurite can form after **lightning** strikes sand.

The air near **lightning** can get five times hotter than the surface of the **Sun**.

A swiftlet, a cave-dwelling bird from Southeast Asia, uses its **spit** to make its **nest**.

Burrowing owls make **nests** in underground burrows they steal from animals like prairie dogs. They sometimes use other animals' **poop** for decoration.

A **poop fossil** is called a coprolite.

Scientists found a 57-million-year-old **fossil** of a **penguin**. When that penguin was alive, it was as tall as an adult human!

Penguins use their sense of **smell** to recognize family members.

The Sun has **tornadoes** that spin at up to 186,000 miles an hour (300,000km/h) —about 600 times faster than the fastest tornadoes recorded on Earth.

A waterspout is a **tornado** that forms in **water** or passes over it.

When a **tick** attaches itself to a host, it creates a glue called cement from its **spit**.

Sand grouses, birds related to pigeons, soak up **water** in their **feathers** for their babies to later wring out and drink.

Scientists have found fossils of dinosaur **feathers** covered in fossilized parasites, like lice and **ticks**.

Furry friends ›

There are about 300 million **smell** receptors in a **dog**'s nose— humans have about 6 million.

In ancient China, some **dogs** were called "sleeve dogs" because they were small enough to carry around in the sleeve of a robe.

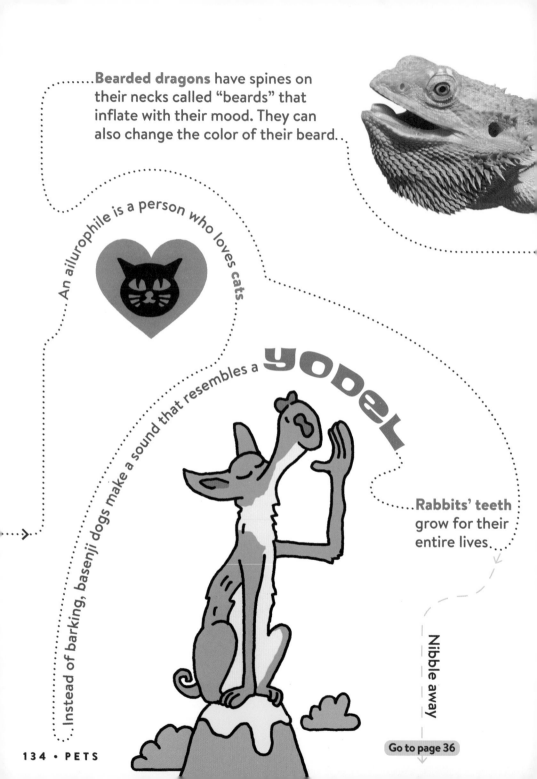

Bearded dragons have spines on their necks called "beards" that inflate with their mood. They can also change the color of their beard.

An ailurophile is a person who loves cats

Instead of barking, basenji dogs make a sound that resembles a YODEL

Rabbits' teeth grow for their entire lives.

Nibble away

Go to page 36

In ancient China, **goldfish** were symbols of luck and so prized that only members of the royal family could own them....

Pan for gold

The ocean holds nearly 14 tons (12,700kg) of dissolved **GOLD**

Scientists think some of **Earth's gold** may have come from space

The James Webb Space Telescope has **18 mirrors**, each covered with a microscopic layer of gold.

Pyrite also goes by the name "fool's gold," because it looks just like the precious metal. You can test whether you have pyrite or real gold by striking it with something metallic—fool's gold gives off **sparks**, while real gold does not.

Gotcha!

One ounce (28g) of gold can be STRETCHED into a microscopic wire 50 miles (80km) long.

Decorator crabs cover themselves in rocks, corals, or even animals like anemones and sea urchins, as **camouflage**. Velcro-like hairs hold their ocean accessories in place

Frogfish have **lures** on the tops of their heads that look like wiggling worms to entice other fish to get close enough to be gobbled up...

Mimic octopuses can change color, but they can also change their **body shape** to impersonate several different kinds of animal, like crabs, sea snakes, even seahorses...

Now you see it

It can take just 13 milliseconds for the **brain** to process what you see.

Your **brain**'s **electrical** signals can travel up to 270 miles an hour (435km/h)— that's speedier than the world's fastest train.

The world's largest model **ship** in a bottle is contained inside a glass **bottle** so big an adult can stand inside.

Scientists have discovered **plastic**-eating **bacteria**.

A **bottle** made of **plastic** can take more than 450 years to decompose.

The **electrical** current that flows through an outlet in your home is less powerful than one species of electric **eel**, which can use 860 volts of electricity to shock its prey.

A **knot** is a unit of speed for a **ship**.

Moray **eels** can tie themselves into **knots**.

Roll out the paper! ·····>

Bacteria can travel up to six feet (1.8m) through the air after you flush the **toilet** with the lid open.

The earliest known use of **toilet** paper was in sixth-century China. It was made out of hemp, rice, and even paper that scholars had written on.

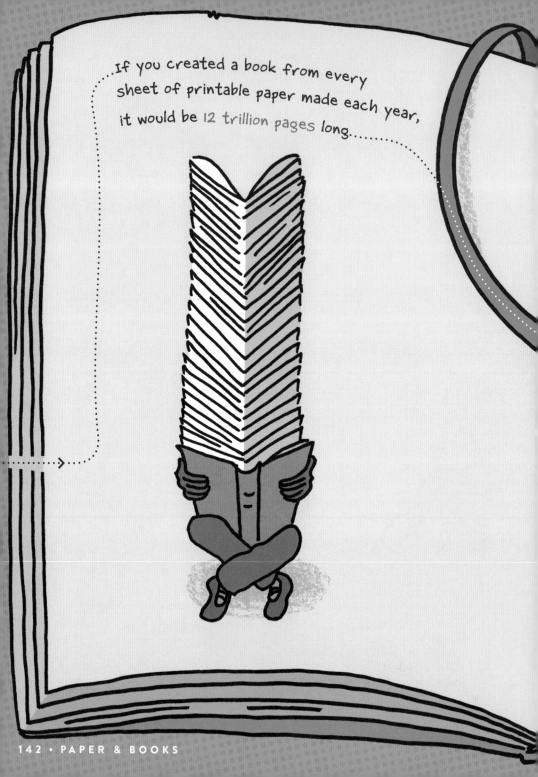

If you created a book from every sheet of printable paper made each year, it would be 12 trillion pages long.

The Voynich manuscript is a 600-year-old mysterious book illustrated with dragons, castles, plants, and more drawings. It's also written in an ancient or **coded language** that historians and even code breakers haven't been able to decipher.

Now you're talking

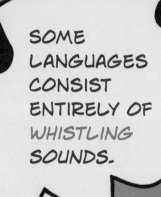

SOME LANGUAGES CONSIST ENTIRELY OF *WHISTLING* SOUNDS.

THERE ARE MORE THAN 7,000 LANGUAGES SPOKEN AROUND THE WORLD.

Listen up

Go to page 194

Identical twins are not entirely identical: They don't have the same fingerprints

Slooowwwly

Two-toed sloths, named after the twin claws on each front foot, are one of the slowest animals on Earth—so slow that algae grows on their fur.

The planet Venus has the slowest spin in the Solar System—

it makes a full revolution once every 243 Earth days

Seahorses are some of the world's slowest swimmers—only moving about 5 feet (1.5m) every hour.

Speed it up! →

A blue whale's heart can beat as slowly as two beats per minute.

The world's fastest bathtub, mounted onto a go-kart, hit speeds of 118 miles an hour (190km/h).

Bertie is the world's fastest **tortoise.** He has been clocked at speeds of 0.92 feet per second (0.28m/s).

The fastest-spinning **planet** ever discovered, Beta Pictoris b, has an eight-hour day—it turns at a speed of 56,000 miles an hour (90,000km/h). By comparison, Earth spins at only about 1,000 miles an hour (1,609km/h).

We're losing time!

The higher up you are, the faster **time** passes

The light from **Proxima Centauri**—the next closest star

Cleopatra lived closer to the year the first Pizza Hut opened than the year the Great Pyramid at Giza was completed

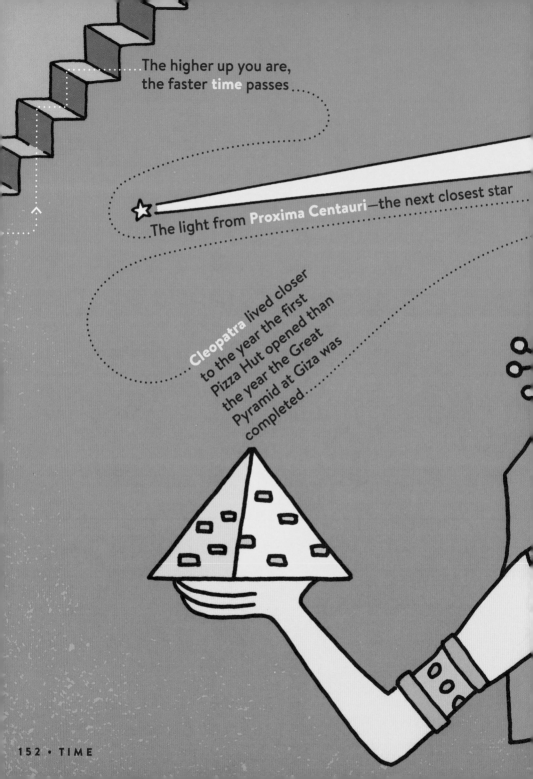

Go to page 84

Time to fly!

after the Sun—takes just over four years to reach Earth.

......When you see or experience something new or unexpected, time might seem like it's passing by more slowly. Scientists call this the **oddball** effect...

...During the reign of the dinosaurs, a year was **370 days** long.

What a year!

Go to page 8

...>.....You shed your entire outer layer
of **skin** up to 26 times each year.

A fresh start

About 130 million babies are born

Experts estimate there
are about 500,000
earthquakes around
the world that they can
...detect each year.........

.....You **blink** more than 10.5 million
times a year. Scientists think
blinking actually does more
than just keep our eyeballs
wet—it helps our brain
refocus its attention.

every year—that's 250 babies a minute.

Zzzzzz...

Every year, you'll spend an average of 3,000 hours asleep—but that's much less than a koala, which spends more than 6,500 hours sleeping!

Z Z Z

Bottlenose dolphins sleep with one eye open

...If you use an

ALARM CLOCK

to wake up, you will likely have a harder
time remembering your dream...

Ssshhh!

About 12 percent of people dream in black and white.

Splash some color ....

There's a species of lizard in Papua New Guinea that has

GREEN BLOOD

Flamingos get their pink coloring from the shrimp, crabs, and algae they eat.

Go to page 124

I see, I see

Heterochromia iridis is when a person or animal has two **different-colored eyes**

Some **octopuses** change color while they sleep.

Munch munch

Rainbow Mountain or the "Mountain of Seven Colors" in Peru has **stripes** of gold, turquoise, red, and purple.

Over the rainbow

Go to page 188

A MOONBOW IS A RAINBOW THAT OCCURS

SOME ANCIENT AUSTRALIAN CULTURES BELIEVED

EVERY RAINBOW HAS A SECOND, FAINTLY

RAINBOW FALLS IN HAWAII IS FAMOUS FOR ITS RAINBOWS,

IN NORSE MYTHOLOGY, A RAINBOW BRIDGE, CALLED BIFROST,

THE LONGEST-LASTING RAINBOW

RAINBOWS NEVER END BECAUSE THEY ARE CIRCLES.

FROM THE LIGHT REFLECTED BY THE MOON

THAT A GIANT RAINBOW SERPENT SHAPED THE LAND

COLORED RAINBOW VISIBLE ON TOP OF THE FIRST

WHICH FORM FROM THE MIST OF THE WATERFALL

CONNECTS THE HUMAN WORLD WITH THE LAND OF THE GODS

WAS VISIBLE FOR ALMOST 9 HOURS

SOMETIMES YOU CAN SEE THE ENTIRE CIRCLE FROM AN AIRCRAFT

Round and round!

In the deserts of Namibia, Africa, are

A pattern's emerging

thousands of polka-dot-like patterns of circular rings of grass called "fairy circles." Scientists aren't quite sure what causes them.

Giraffe **spot** patterns, which help the animals blend into their savanna homes, are passed down from mother to baby...

The five-dot pattern that appears on items like dice is called a quincunx...

Fractals are repeating patterns that appear over and over at different sizes and scales. Broccoli, coastlines, tree bark, and snowflakes are all examples of fractals.

Let it snow! ········>>

......> A snowflake consists of multiple snow crystals that stick together. Every winter, scientists estimate

1,000,000,000,000,

Brrrr! →

000,000,000,000

(1 septillion)
snow crystals
fall from the sky...

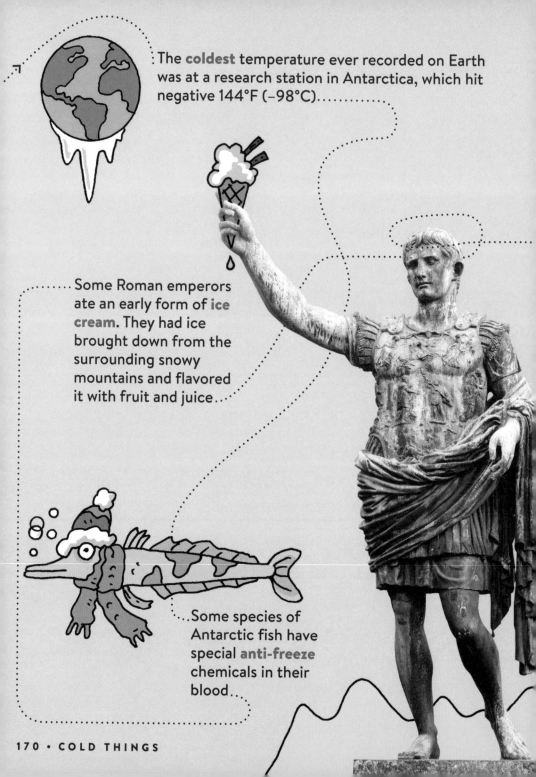

The **coldest** temperature ever recorded on Earth was at a research station in Antarctica, which hit negative 144°F (–98°C).

Some Roman emperors ate an early form of **ice cream**. They had ice brought down from the surrounding snowy mountains and flavored it with fruit and juice.

Some species of Antarctic fish have special **anti-freeze** chemicals in their blood.

When thunder and lightning happen during a snowstorm, it's called

THUNDERSNOW.

It's heating up!

Scientists think Titan, one of Saturn's moons, has volcanoes that erupt ice

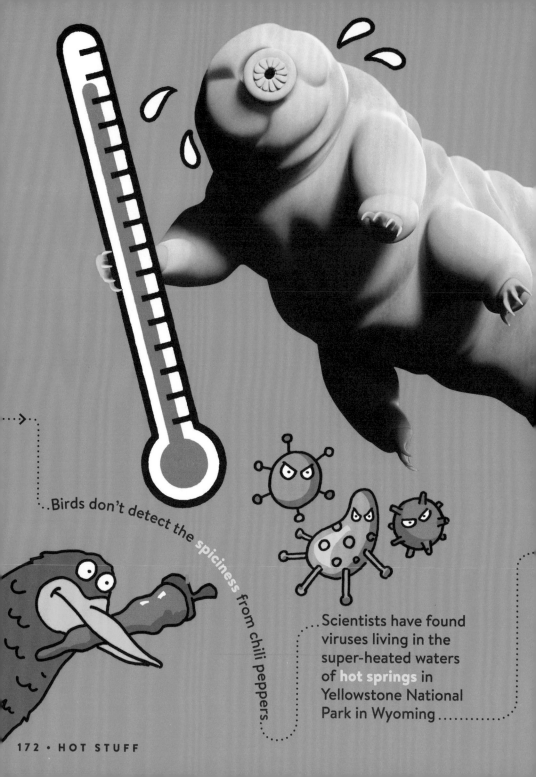

...Birds don't detect the spiciness from chili peppers.

Scientists have found viruses living in the super-heated waters of **hot springs** in Yellowstone National Park in Wyoming......

When a massive star dies, its core temperature can soar **billions of degrees**, then the star explodes in an event called a supernova.

Dry as a desert

Tardigrades, also called moss piglets or water bears, are only half a millimeter long and can survive in **boiling** water.

The world's largest **hot desert** is the Sahara in Africa, which has vast seas of shifting sands called ergs.

Reach for the stars

Go to page 178

Scientists think that by studying super-dry deserts like Chile's Atacama Desert, they can uncover clues of how life could survive on **Mars**.

Mars has **blue** sunsets.

Blue morpho butterflies aren't actually blue—they look blue to us because special ridges on their **wing** scales reflect blue light.

A Komodo **dragon**, the world's largest lizard, secretes a powerful venom from glands in its mouth, allowing it to kill prey the size of a **buffalo**.

Some Viking **ships** had **dragon** heads carved onto the front.

The hard spot where an African cape **buffalo's horns** meet is called a "boss."

Male bighorn sheep have **horns** that can weigh up to 30 pounds (14kg)—heavier than all the **bones** in its body combined.

The **bones** of all flying **birds** are hollow.

Some arctic **foxes** live in dens that are more than **100** years old.

The **wings** of flying **foxes**, the world's largest bats, can measure up to 6 feet (1.8m) across—nearly the length of a full-size bed!

There are **100** tiles in the **game** of Scrabble™.

Egyptian pharaohs were buried with everything they would need for the **afterlife**—Pharaoh Khufu, who built the Great Pyramid at Giza, was buried with a 144-foot-long (43.9m-long) **ship**.

One of the world's oldest board **games** is called Senet. Popular in ancient Egypt, the game symbolized the journey to the **afterlife**.

I ♥ ♥ facts

Some **bird** species cover themselves in ants. Scientists think birds may use the chemicals the **ants** release to deter other insects, like an insect-repellent.

An **ant's** heart is shaped like a tube.

Burmese pythons' **HEARTS** grow up to 40 percent larger after eating a big **MEAL.** Some have been known to eat big animals such as crocodiles.

Twinkle, twinkle ⟩

The Heart Nebula's red color and heart shape result from the activity of a cluster of stars at its center

Octopuses have three hearts

STARS

don't actually **twinkle**.

Earth's atmosphere distorts stars' light, in what's called "scintillation"

..There's a giant **diamond** located 50 light-years from Earth that scientists estimate is 10 billion trillion trillion carats. It's the core of an old star...................

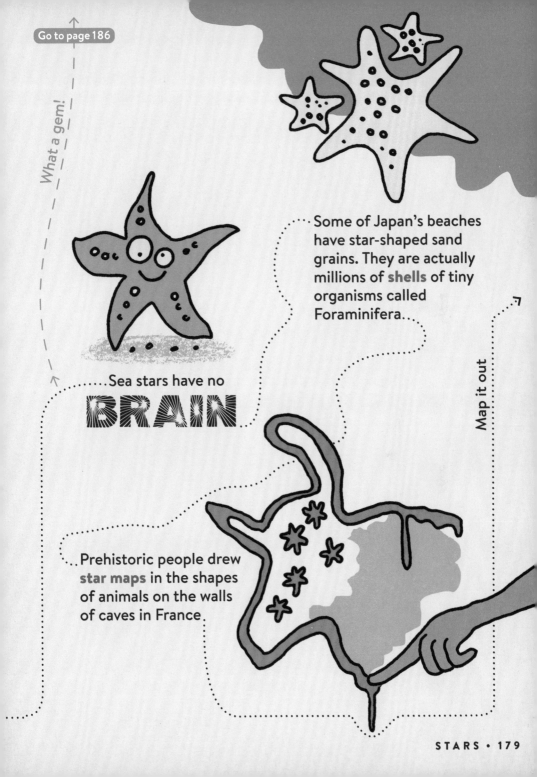

Go to page 186

What a gem!

Some of Japan's beaches have star-shaped sand grains. They are actually millions of **shells** of tiny organisms called Foraminifera.

Sea stars have no

BRAIN

Map it out

Prehistoric people drew **star maps** in the shapes of animals on the walls of caves in France.

NASA has sent a map into space to show **extraterrestrial life** how to get to Earth

To catch people copying their work, some mapmakers put **fake** towns or streets on their maps, called paper towns and trap streets...

Look both ways!

Every year, residents of Dunedin, New Zealand, race 25,000 red candies down Baldwin Street, the world's steepest street.

The first basketball **net** was made out of a **peach** basket.

Humpback whales sometimes blow **bubbles** while swimming in circles, creating a bubble **net** to trap and catch their prey.

The world's largest **peach** is in South Carolina. Called the Peachoid, it is actually a **water** tower that can hold 1 million gallons (3.7 million liters) of water.

A **New Zealand sheep** named Shrek was lost for six years. When he was found, he had grown enough wool to make 20 men's suits.

Sheep can recognize and remember human **faces**.

The **face** with **tears** of joy is the world's most popular emoji.

Some parrotfish species sleep inside a **mucus bubble** that they make from an organ in their head. This slimy cocoon protects them from parasites.

Your **tears** contain **mucus.**

It's raining!

A blood rain is when the **water** that falls from the sky appears red or brown. Scientists think the strange weather phenomenon is caused by dust from deserts that mixes with the water in clouds.

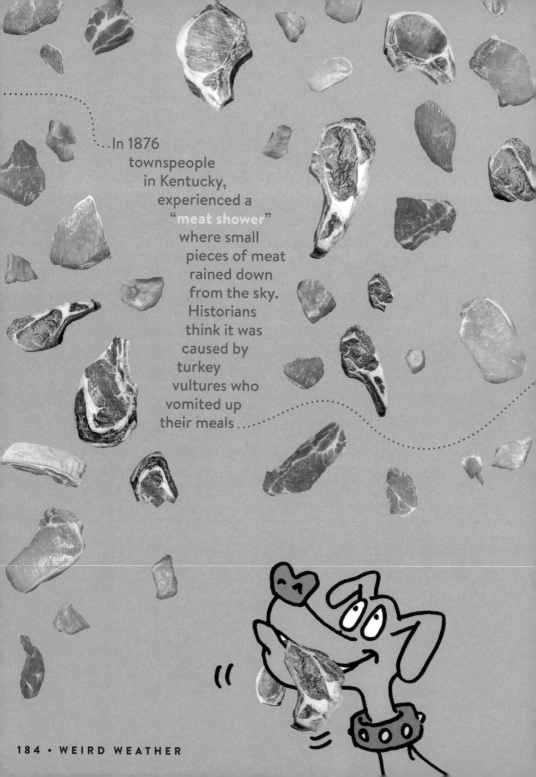

...In 1876 townspeople in Kentucky, experienced a "**meat shower**" where small pieces of meat rained down from the sky. Historians think it was caused by turkey vultures who vomited up their meals...

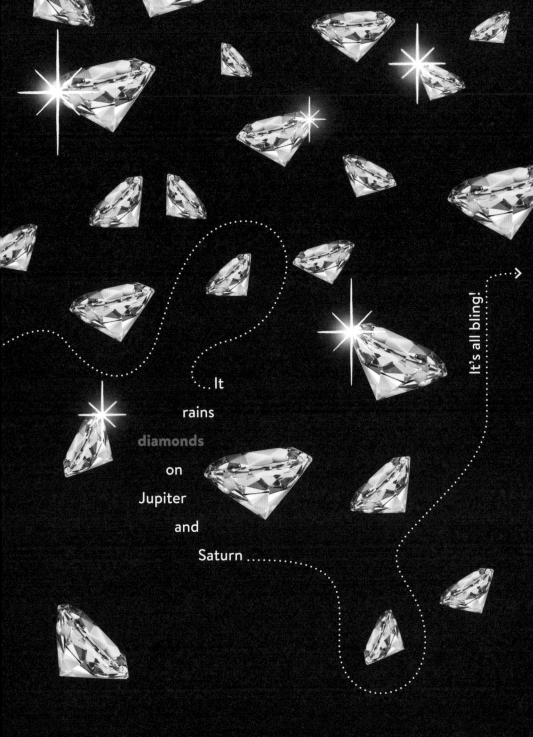

It rains **diamonds** on Jupiter and Saturn

It's all bling!

The ancient Greeks and Romans thought diamonds were **tears** from the gods.

A dog named

Honey Bun

accidentally ate $10,000 worth of diamonds from her owner's jewelry store. The diamonds came out safely from the other end.

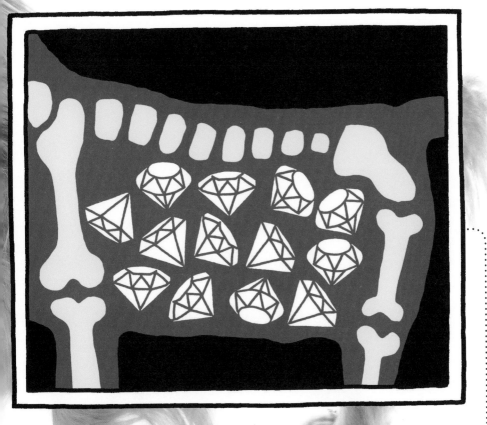

Snacktime!

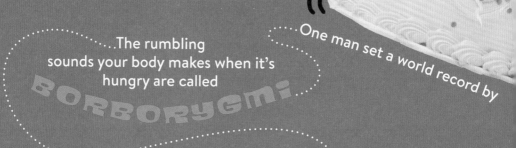

...The rumbling sounds your body makes when it's hungry are called **BORBORYGMI**...

One man set a world record by

Animals that **eat their own poop**, such as guinea pigs and rabbits, are called coprophages...

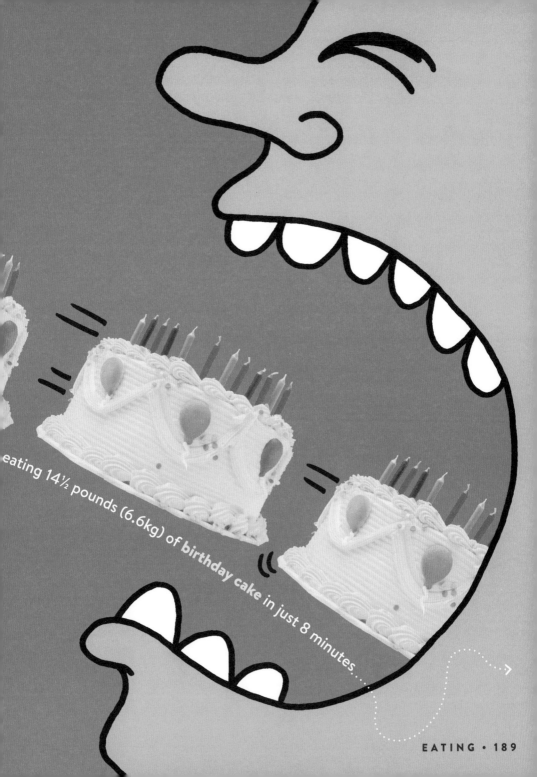

eating 14½ pounds (6.6kg) of birthday cake in just 8 minutes...

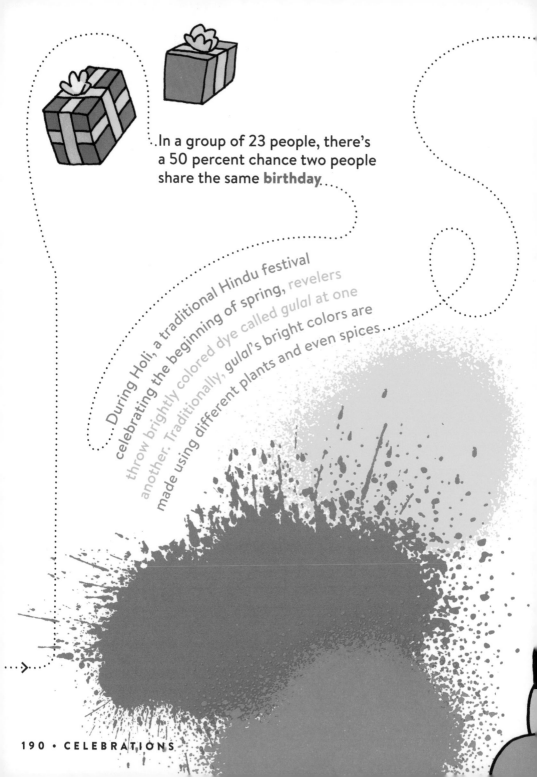

In a group of 23 people, there's a 50 percent chance two people share the same **birthday**.

During Holi, a traditional Hindu festival celebrating the beginning of spring, revelers throw brightly colored dye called *gulal* at one another. Traditionally, *gulal*'s bright colors are made using different plants and even spices.

Thousands of pounds of fruit are arranged in towers during Thailand's **Monkey Buffet Festival**, where macaque monkeys are the guests of honor.

You can go mud-skiing, get your face painted with mud, or speed down a mud slide at South Korea's Boryeong

MUD FESTIVAL,

which celebrates the area's mineral-rich earth.

Every **New Year's Eve**, Australia's Sydney Harbor lights up with more than 36,000 fireworks.

Whoosh!

Different chemicals in fireworks cause different sounds:

titanium makes a loud **BOOM**

Listen up! →

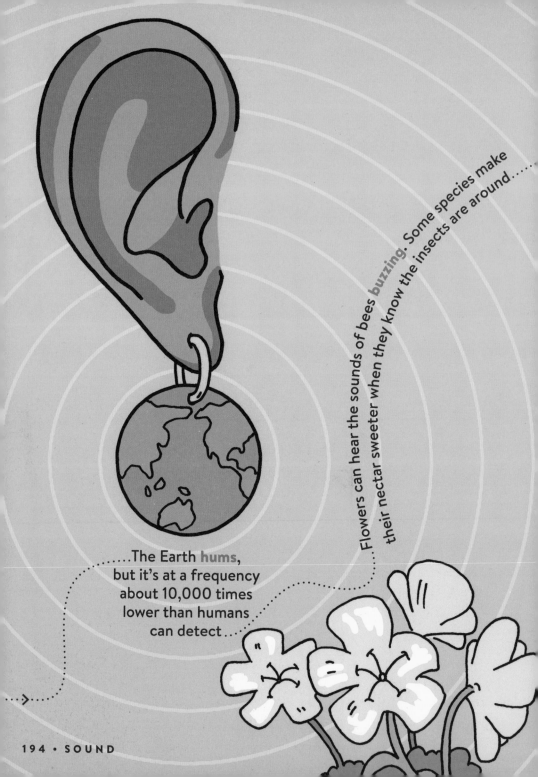

Flowers can hear the sounds of bees **buzzing**. Some species make their nectar sweeter when they know the insects are around......

.....The Earth **hums**, but it's at a frequency about 10,000 times lower than humans can detect....

La-lala-di-dah

Sharks like the sounds of heavy metal music

An **underwater music festival** is held every year in Florida. Some festivalgoers "play" fish-themed instruments along to music from underwater speakers.

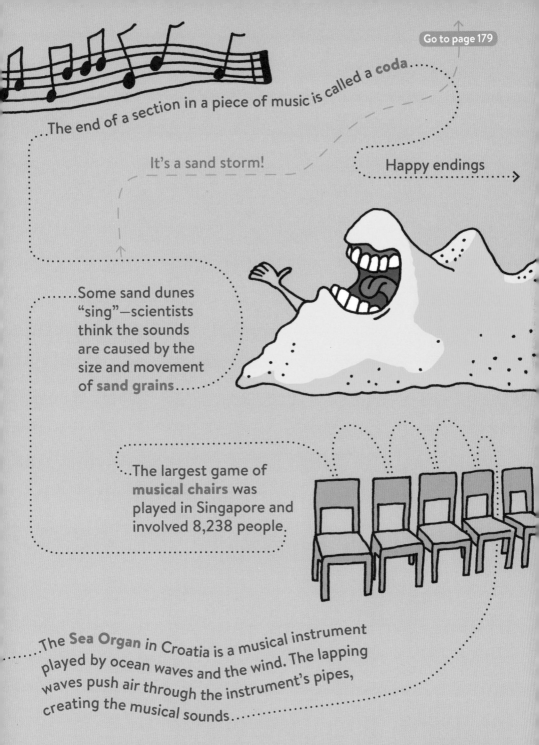

Go to page 179

The end of a section in a piece of music is called a **coda**.

It's a sand storm!

Happy endings

Some sand dunes "sing"—scientists think the sounds are caused by the size and movement of **sand grains**.

The largest game of **musical chairs** was played in Singapore and involved 8,238 people.

The **Sea Organ** in Croatia is a musical instrument played by ocean waves and the wind. The lapping waves push air through the instrument's pipes, creating the musical sounds.

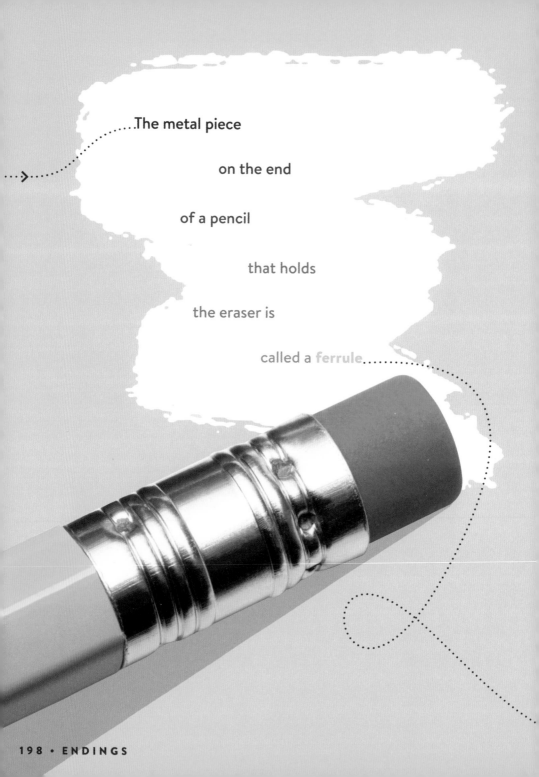

The metal piece

on the end

of a pencil

that holds

the eraser is

called a ferrule.

Go to page 50

Keep circling

.....The record for most alternative
endings to a book is **1,250**, in the
book *Wonder Crystal*. All of the
different endings were written by kids_

Index

Trademark notices

Mr. Potato Head is a trademark of Hasbro, Inc
LEGO is a trademark of the LEGO Group
Barbie is a trademark of Mattel, Inc
Slinky is a trademark of POOF-SLINKY, INC
Play-Doh is a trademark of Hasbro, Inc

Formula 1 is a trademark of Formula One
Licensing B.V.
Velcro is a trademark of Velcro Companies
Pizza Hut is a trademark of Pizza Hut, Inc.
Scrabble is a trademark of Hasbro, Inc.

Meet the FACTopians

Kate Hale is an author, editor, and professional fun fact finder based in Alexandria, Virginia, USA. She has edited or written about everything from how dogs communicate to biographies of inspiring scientists. When thinking about which fun facts to include in *FACTopia*, Kate took inspiration from everywhere—from her favorite animals (rabbits and giraffes) to her breakfast (eggs... and maybe a doughnut or two). Her favorite fact in this book is that the giant squid has a brain shaped like a doughnut.

Andy Smith is an award-winning illustrator. A graduate of the Royal College of Art, London, UK, he creates artwork which has an optimistic, hand-made feel. When creating the illustrations for *FACTopia*, he really enjoyed the surprise that every page would bring—he could never predict what he'd be drawing next! He particularly enjoyed drawing the chimpanzee on page 37, whose smile felt quite infectious.

Lawrence Morton is an art director and designer based in London, UK. Designing this book reminded him of the myth of Theseus on his quest through the labyrinth. Lawrence created a trail of dots through the pages to help the reader navigate safely on their adventure through *FACTopia*. His favorite fact in this book is that dogs understand about 165 human words (though he thinks his dachshund Charley knows even more than that).

Sources

Scientists and other experts are discovering new facts and updating information all the time. That's why our *FACTopia* team has checked that every fact that appears in this book is based on multiple trustworthy sources and has been verified by a team of Britannica fact-checkers. Of the hundreds of sources used in this book, here is a list of key websites we consulted.

News Organizations
abcnews.go.com
theatlantic.com
bbc.co.uk
bbc.com
cnn.com
discovermagazine.com
theguardian.com
latimes.com
nationalgeographic.com
nationalgeographic.org
nbcnews.com
nytimes.com
popularmechanics.com
reuters.com
sciencefocus.com
scientificamerican.com
slate.com
time.com
washingtonpost.com
wired.com
usatoday.com

Government, Scientific, and Academic Organizations
sciencemag.org
acs.org
audubon.org
academic.eb.com
britannica.com
jstor.org
merriam-webster.com
nature.com
nasa.gov
ncbi.nlm.nih.gov
noaa.gov
nps.gov
oceanexplorer.noaa.gov
usgs.gov

Museums and Zoos
amnh.org
nationalzoo.si.edu
ocean.si.edu
si.edu
smithsonianmag.com

Universities
animaldiversity.org
harvard.edu
oregonstate.edu

Other Websites
atlasobscura.com
dkfindout.com
guinnessworldrecords.com
nwf.org
pbs.org
ripleys.com
sciencedaily.com
worldatlas.com

Picture Credits

The publisher would like to thank the following for permission to reproduce their photographs and illustrations.

Key: top (t), bottom (b)

p.12 Alamy/blickwinkel; p.13 Getty/James Johnstone/500px; p.14–15 Alamy/agefotostock; p.18 iStock/Spanic; p.19 Alamy/Valentyn Volkov; p.20 Alamy/Michael Runkel; p.23 Getty/Image Source; p.24 Getty/dszc; p.26–27 iStock/Martin Barraud; p.28–29 Alamy/Ferenc Ungor; p.31 Getty/Jason Webber Photography; p.32–33 Getty/Jean-Daniel Ketting EyeEm; p.34–35 iStock/reptiles4all; p.36 iStock/Freder; p.39 Alamy/Image Source; p.40 Getty/Jamie Yan/EyeEm; p.42 Getty/George D. Lepp; p.44 Getty/National Science Foundation; p.46–47 Alamy/Erik Schlogl; p.50–51 Getty/Vitalij Cerepok/EyeEm; p.52 NASA; p.54–55 iStock/sofiaworld; p.55t Alamy/Alfio Scisetti; p.57 Dreamstime/Artushfoto; p.58 Getty/ewald mario; p.60–61 Getty/Exotica.im/Universal Images Group; p.62–63 iStock/spooh; p.64 Alamy/vkstudio; p.66–67 iStock/zhaojiankang; p.68 Getty/Frank Bienewald/LightRocket; p.70–71 iStock/tiero; p.73 Nature Picture Library/Tim MacMillan/John Downer Pro; p.74–75 Getty/sinopics; p.77 Alamy/Avalon/Photoshot Licence; p.78 Getty/Fadil; p.81 Getty/Alexandra Rudge; p.82 Alamy/mauritius images GmbH; p.84–85 iStock/kickers; p.86–87 Getty/Sean Gladwell; p.88–89 123rf.com/titonz; p.90–91 123rf.com/freestyledesignworks; p.92–93 Alamy/amana images inc.; p.94 Alamy/Patti McConville; p.95 123rf.com/Konstantin Kopachinsky; p.97 iStock/Catherine Withers-Clarke; p.98–99 123rf.com/andreykuzim; p.100 Alamy/Life on White; p.103 Alamy/SuperStock; p.105 Getty/Jorge Guerrero/AFP; p.106–107 Getty/Heritage Images; p.108–109 Getty/da-kuk; p.110 Dreamstime/Vladimirfloyd; p.113 Dreamstime/Kzeniya Ragozina; p.114 Alamy/Richard Dirscherl; p.115 123rf.com/andreykuzim; p.116–117 Nature Picture Library/Doc White; p.118 Getty/jasonganzmd; p.119 iStock/PeopleImages; p.120 iStock/daneger; p.122–123 iStock/rancho_runner; p.124 Alamy/Gilberto Mesquita; p.125 Getty/WestEnd61; p.126 iStock/Marius Ltu; p.129 Getty/Ger Bosma; p.130–131 123rf.com/Ian Dixon; p.134 Dreamstime/Susan Leggett; p.135 Getty/JimmyJamesBond; p.136–137 Getty/Tim Graham; p.138–139 Nature Picture Library/Gary Bell/Oceanwide; p.143 Beinecke Rare Book and Manuscript Library; p.144 Alamy/leonello calvetti; p.147 Nature Picture Library/Michael Durham; p.148 Alamy/Martin; p.149 Alamy/shufu; p.150–151 Alamy/Science Photo Library; p.153 iStock/Portugal2004; p.155 Getty/Ali Saadat/EyeEm; p.156 Alamy/Redmond Durrell; p.159 Alamy/Sarayuth Punnasuriyaporn; p.160 Alamy/Daniel L. Geiger/SNAP; p.160–161 Dreamstime/Ionut David; p.164–165 Alamy/Robert Harding; p.167 iStock/marcoventuriniautieri; p.168–169 iStock/borchee; p.170 iStock/AndreaAstes; p.171t Dreamstime/Vitalii Kit; p.171b Dreamstime/Valentyn75; p.172–173 Dreamstime/Planetfelicity; p.177 Nature Picture Library/Alex Mustard; p.178 Alamy/E R Degginger; p.180–181 NASA; p.184 iStock/milanfoto; p.184 Getty/ATU Images; p.185 Getty/Ryan McVay; p.186–187 Alamy/YAY Media AS; p.188–189 Dreamstime/Denis Mishalov; p.191 Getty/Jason Miller; p.192–193 Getty/Peter Saloutous; p.195 iStock/Antagain; p.196 Getty/Rick Neves; p.198 iStock/t_kimura.

BRITANNICA
BOOKS

Britannica Books is an imprint of What on Earth Publishing,
published in collaboration with Britannica, Inc.
Allington Castle, Maidstone, Kent ME16 0NB, United Kingdom
30 Ridge Road Unit B, Greenbelt, Maryland, 20770, United States

First published in the United States in 2021

Written by Kate Hale
Illustrated by Andy Smith
Designed by Lawrence Morton
Edited by Judy Barratt
Indexed by Vanessa Bird

Encyclopaedia Britannica
Alison Eldridge, Managing Editor; Michele Rita Metych and R.E. Green, Fact Checkers

Britannica Books
Nancy Feresten, Publisher; Natalie Bellos, Executive Editor; Andy Forshaw, Art Director;
Alenka Oblak, Production Manager

ISBN: 9781912920716

Printed in China

1 3 5 7 9 10 8 6 4 2

whatonearthbooks.com
books.britannica.com